RECONSIDERING
COLLEGE

RECONSIDERING COLLEGE

Christian Higher Education for Working Adults

RICK OSTRANDER

Abilene Christian University Press

RECONSIDERING COLLEGE

Christian Higher Education for Working Adults

ACU
PRESS

Copyright 2014 by Rick Ostrander

ISBN 978-0-89112-398-9

Printed in the United States of America

Scripture quotations, unless otherwise noted, are from The Holy Bible, New International Version. Copyright 1984, International Bible Society. Used by permission of Zondervan Publishers.

Cover design by Rick Gibson
Interior text design by Sandy Armstrong, Strong Design

For information contact:
Abilene Christian University Press
1626 Campus Court
Abilene, Texas 79601

1-877-816-4455 toll free
www.acupressbooks.com

14 15 16 17 18 19 20 / 7 6 5 4 3 2 1

CONTENTS

PREFACE

THERE was a time in the not too distant past when "going to college" was associated almost exclusively with the young adult years. In the popular mind, college was that time of life when you graduated from high school, packed your Honda full of clothes, books, and a Frisbee, and headed off to State University for four years of school before embarking on adulthood. And while that mentality stills exists, the reality in the United States is quite different. According to the National Student Clearinghouse Research Center, in 2012 thirty-eight percent of all college students were twenty-five years or older. As our economy continues to change, more and more adults are seeking to improve themselves and their professional opportunities by completing a college degree.[1]

I can attest from personal experience both to the sacrifice and the rewards of education in the adult years. I married my wife at the relatively young age of twenty-one, after attending Bible college for three years. After working for a telecommunications software company while my wife completed her

According to the National Student Clearinghouse Research Center, in 2012 thirty-eight percent of all college students were twenty-five years or older.

master's degree, I decided that I belonged in academia as a profession. So we packed up our few possessions and headed to Ann Arbor, Michigan, where I completed my bachelor's degree in history. From there we headed to South Bend, Indiana, where I began the long, arduous journey of earning master's and doctoral degrees in American history at the University of Notre Dame. Unlike many graduate students, we also began raising children during the graduate school years. In fact, we had three young children by the time I completed my doctorate.

To help make ends meet, each summer I would put the books away, put on work clothes, and operate a residential painting business with an old college friend. Painting houses during the summer months helped me appreciate the value of books and study; and nine months of academic life would in turn make me appreciate the value of working hard and bringing home a paycheck.

After six years of graduate school, I completed my degree and landed an academic job teaching history at a small Christian college in Arizona. Ironically, my first job in academia brought home less money per week than I had earned as a house painter. I learned much through the experience of juggling the pressures of work, school, and family. Two main lessons stand out. First, some of us are wired by God to strive, learn, and to expand our capacities. Though our culture may value certain professions differently, from a Christian perspective there is nothing inherently better about being a college professor than being a house painter. For myself, however, pursuing graduate study was an important element of my personal and career path, and it has placed me in that "sweet spot" of my talents matching certain needs in society.

Second, I learned the value of following one's passion in life and trusting that God has a purpose in it, even when one cannot always see the practical benefit. As I neared completion of my PhD and began sending out job letters, the typical response I received was, "Thank you for your interest. We have received three hundred applications for this position and will be working our way through them in the next few months." Needless to say, it was a discouraging position to be in, and several times I questioned whether I had made the right decision in following God's leading to graduate school. My father-in-law, ever the practical sort, wondered whether it might not make more sense in supporting my family to abandon my attempts to break into academia and stick with painting

> If we follow what we believe to be God's calling on our lives and develop our gifts and passions, God honors that and places us in roles in which those gifts can be used.

houses. That was a good question indeed, considering the fact that while I dreamed of waxing eloquent in the college classroom, I also had three young children who needed some basic things like food and shoes.

In my case things turned out fairly well, and my first teaching job, while not lucrative, did prove to be an important first step in a career in academia. And while not every "starving graduate student" story turns out like mine did, I have become convinced that if we follow what we believe to be God's calling on our lives and develop our gifts and passions, God honors that and places us in roles in which those gifts can be used. In the Sermon on the Mount, Jesus told his followers not to worry about physical needs such as food and clothing. Instead, he said, "Seek first the kingdom of God and his righteousness, and all these things will be given to you as well."

> This book is designed to help you understand the value of adult education, and explain some ways that such an education can be distinctively Christian.

For many Christians in today's society, seeking first God's kingdom—and our place in advancing that kingdom here on earth—will involve pursuing education amid a busy schedule of work, family, church, and community life. But the struggle is well worth it.[2]

This short book is about the value of Christian higher education for the working adult. Whether you are a painter, bookkeeper, salesperson, mother, nurse, or engaged in any other profession, you probably recognize the value of furthering your education—even if that is simply an instinctive hunch rather than a deliberate calculation. This book is designed to help you understand the value of adult education, and explain some ways that such an education can be distinctively Christian. But first, we will begin by discussing a Christian perspective on work.

Chapter 1

WORK IS WORSHIP

The Value of Labor in the Christian Life

THIS book is primarily about the value of education to the working adult. But if our education is in some way connected to our career—and for most of us, that is the case—then we cannot adequately understand the value of education unless we have a proper Christian understanding of work as more than simply a way to earn a living. As this chapter will explain, work, for the Christian, is both a way to glorify our Creator by doing what we were designed to do and a way to help bring healing and order to a fallen world.

One of my earliest encounters with the value of work was not a pleasant one. As a sixth-grader growing up in suburban Chicago, I developed a brief infatuation with procuring candy bars from the shelves of the local 7-Eleven. Eventually I got caught and my parents were notified. My punishment was that I had to spend an entire Saturday cleaning the house, including vacuuming floors, scrubbing shower tiles, and washing windows. Surprisingly, by day's end I had come to take

> Work, for the Christian, is both a way to glorify our Creator by doing what we were designed to do and a way to help bring healing and order to a fallen world.

a certain amount of satisfaction in what I had accomplished, and how different a bathroom floor looked after an hour's worth of elbow grease applied to it. My mother remarked afterward that she was impressed by the sense of diligence that I applied to the various projects—though she also hoped that the experience would cure me of the desire to steal candy from convenience stores.

Looking back, it's clear that I had experienced a quality that our Creator has placed deep in the human soul: A sense of pride and satisfaction in the accomplishment of a task. For the Christian, work is not simply a way to make a living; it's a way to glorify our Creator by performing with excellence what we were created to do.

The dignity of human work is rooted in the Bible. The book of Genesis narrates the creation of Adam and Eve, then it says, "God blessed them and said to them, 'Be fruitful and increase in number; fill the earth and subdue it. Rule over the fish of the sea and the birds of the air and over every living creature that moves on the ground.'" A few verses later the text states: "The Lord God took the man and put him in the Garden of Eden to work it and take care of it." One of the astounding truths of Genesis 1 and 2, in fact, is that God gives

Adam and Eve tremendous responsibilities to rule over and care for his creation.[3]

A good ruler, of course, does not just sit on a throne. The ruler actively *develops* the kingdom—bringing improvements, solving disputes, and increasing prosperity. And that is the privilege God entrusted to humans. From the very beginning, humans were expected to bring changes to creation. Some sort of transformation was to take place as part of cultivating and caring for the earth. Theologians refer to this task as the "cultural mandate"—that God created humans not only to enjoy and steward his creation, but to develop it, even to transform it. Consider the opposite end of the Bible, the book of Revelation. This book tells us that the culmination of God's redemptive work will not be another garden but rather a city—and not an ordinary city but one with walls decorated with precious jewels, streets of gold, and full of gardens and vineyards. If Genesis depicts a creation as simple and harmonious as a Bach cello solo, Revelation describes a complex, multi-layered creation like that of a Beethoven symphony. This transformation to creation occurs in part through human labor.

That's why throughout the Old Testament, meaningful work is praised as a sign of God's blessing and a mark of obedience to him. For example, in Psalm 128, the Psalmist states that the ability to enjoy the fruit of one's labor is a sign of God's blessings. Passages praising work and condemning laziness are sprinkled throughout the book of Proverbs (as those of us who grew up in Sunday school can attest), such

> Throughout the Old Testament, meaningful work is praised as a sign of God's blessing and a mark of obedience to him.

as that found in Proverbs 14:23: "Hard work brings a profit, but mere talk leads only to poverty." Clearly, human work that brings changes and improvements to creation is an expression of who we are as created in God's image.

Of course, work has not always been viewed positively throughout human history. In fact, one of the revolutionary changes that Christianity brought to the Classical civilization of its day was a re-valuing of the dignity of labor. Greece and Rome were slave societies in which the tasks of food production and daily life were generally bestowed on slaves and other manual laborers so that "true" men could devote their time to politics, culture, fighting wars, and pleasure. In fact, the term "liberal arts" originated in the educational program of men who were "liberated" from the constraints both of political tyranny and of manual labor so that they could engage in the activities appropriate to free men. The reason that Socrates and others could discuss philosophy in the Athens city square was because others were busy growing food, making clothes, and constructing buildings.

Into this culture, Jesus, the Son of God, came as the son of a Nazarene carpenter and learned to swing a hammer. He recruited disciples from the ranks of doctors, fishermen, and tax collectors. For his parables, Jesus drew lessons from the typical jobs of the day such as farming, building, fishing, and vineyard-tending.

After Jesus's ascension, his followers began spreading the Good News throughout the Roman Empire. The Apostle Paul was an Old Testament scholar, but he was also a tent-maker who earned his own living as he traveled throughout the Roman world. His message took hold primarily among the working classes of the day. As he reminded the Christians in the city of Corinth: "Brothers and sisters, think of what you were when you were called. Not many of you were wise by human standards; not many were influential; not many were of noble birth. But God chose the foolish things of the world to shame the wise; God chose the weak things of the world to shame the strong."[4]

Moreover, while we tend to glorify early Christians such as Paul who traveled around establishing new churches, Paul's instruction to new believers was not to abandon their professions and become full-time missionaries, but rather to stay where they were and work hard. As he told his followers in Thessalonika: "Make it your ambition to lead a quiet life and work with your hands."[5]

In fact, the early Christians influenced—and eventually dominated—the Roman Empire not by seizing control of the government but by working hard, doing their jobs well, loving each other, caring for the poor, and engaging in acts of compassion that attracted the notice of outsiders in a deteriorating society. In a manuscript dated around 150 AD. known as the Epistle of Mathetes, an observer of the day remarked about the

> What made the early Christians so influential in their world was their commitment to doing the simple tasks of everyday life. Being followers of Jesus did not lead them to abandon their careers; it made them better farmers, merchants, and carpenters.

Christians: "Inhabiting Greek as well as barbarian cities, according as the lot of each of them has determined, and following the customs of the natives in respect to clothing, food, and the rest of their ordinary conduct, they display to us their wonderful and confessedly striking method of life." In other words, what made the early Christians so influential in their world was their commitment to doing the simple tasks of everyday life. Being followers of Jesus did not lead them to abandon their careers; it made them better farmers, merchants, and carpenters.[6]

The experience of the early church illustrates a second value of work from a Christian perspective: When we flourish in our area of giftedness and do our jobs well, we not only glorify our creator but influence our culture in positive ways. We can call this the "redemptive" value of work. This concept will be discussed in more detail later, but briefly stated, Christians believe that God is at work even now in bringing redemption and healing to our fallen world. And one of the primary ways that we contribute to God's redemptive purposes is in our professions.

Gabe Lyons summarizes the situation well when he describes Christians as "restorers" who, like a builder remodeling a beautiful but dilapidated mansion, are engaged in making the world what God intended it to be. He writes: "Instead of waiting for God to unveil the new heaven and the new earth, the rest of us can give the world a taste of what God's kingdom is all about—building up, repairing brokenness, showing mercy, reinstating hope, and generally adding value. In this expanded model, everyone plays an essential role." And for many of us, the primary way that we will live out our roles as "restorers" in society is through meaningful work that not only brings us individual fulfillment but that meets a need in the world. As Frederick Buechner has stated, "the place God calls you is where your deep gladness and the world's deep hunger meet."[7]

Let's take a concrete example from the profession of journalism. On the one hand, a Christian journalist will glorify God simply by doing his job well. After all, God created humans to live in community, and one important element of that community is the ability to communicate truth to each other through accurate and compelling stories about the world. Thus, the work

> Christians believe that God is at work even now in bringing redemption and healing to our fallen world. And one of the primary ways that we contribute to God's redemptive purposes is in our professions.

of journalism itself will exercise a positive influence in the world and contribute to human society. The profession has intrinsic value to God.

Furthermore, the Christian journalist will recognize the subtle ways in which his particular corner of creation is "not the way it's supposed to be," in the words of theologian Cornelius Plantinga. For examples, members of the media sometimes highlight the absurd or the trivial in order to gain more audience share. Or they violate ethical standards in order to get a scoop. Thus, the Christian journalist will at times resist the status quo by writing a complex, difficult story that deserves attention despite the lack of potential market share; or by respecting a person's privacy even when that means losing a story. In these little ways, he brings a Christian influence to this particular corner of creation.

Of course, all of this doesn't nullify the importance of personal evangelism in the workplace as well. As was the case in the early church, the results of Christian excellence in the workplace and resistance of the status quo will at times attract the notice of non-Christians and provide opportunities for the verbal proclamation of the gospel. The Christian journalist, therefore, will also articulate his faith in ways that are compelling and relevant to the non-believer in a post-Christian society. All of these ways illustrate the fact that Christianity brings a new sense of vitality to work, not just to earn a living but to influence our culture in significant ways. That was the case for the early church, and for believers today.

As the Roman Empire collapsed and Christianity asserted greater influence in society, one of the unfortunate side effects was the rise of another sort of denigration of human labor, this time on religious grounds. In the Medieval society dominated by the Roman Catholic Church, the bishops, priests, and monks were considered the "really" spiritual ones, while others in society simply worked to earn a living.

> Christianity brings a new sense of vitality to work, not just to earn a living but to influence our culture in significant ways.

The divide was no longer between slave and free, but between those performing "spiritual" tasks and the average layperson. The Medieval philosopher Thomas Aquinas, for example, developed a hierarchy of trades and professions, all of which, he believed, were inferior to the work of church officials.

In the 1500s, the Protestant Reformers stepped into such a world and re-asserted a biblical view of human labor. Martin Luther protested, among other things, the veneration of the clergy as a special class of society. His book *The Freedom of the Christian* praised manual labor as a calling just as holy as that of preaching a sermon or administering communion. His fellow Reformer John Calvin wrote in the *Institutes of the Christian Religion* that "there is no employment so mean and sordid as not to appear truly respectable, and be deemed highly important in the sight of God."[8]

The followers of Luther and Calvin tended to be middle-class, hardworking individuals who engaged in farming, trade, skilled crafts, and other businesses. One such group of sober, hardworking Protestants known as Puritans established a colony in North America in the 1600s. As the primary educators of early America, the Puritans transmitted their emphasis on the dignity of work to the new nation. Thus, it is no accident that to this day, the "Protestant work ethic" is deeply embedded in American society. Indeed, wherever one finds Christians who take their biblical calling seriously, one will find a willingness to work hard and do one's job well as an important way to glorify our Creator.

Of course, in our day, Paul's admonition to "work with your hands" need not always be interpreted in a literal sense. In the modern global economy in which the creation and management of information is as important as the production of objects, one can follow Paul's instructions to work faithfully by designing buildings, meeting with clients, or processing insurance claims. Sitting behind a desk is no more valuable than working as a plumber; but in today's world there are a greater variety of ways to honor God with our work than were available to the Christians in Paul's day.

> Wherever one finds Christians who take their biblical calling seriously, one will find a willingness to work hard and do one's job well as an important way to glorify our Creator.

As a Christian, therefore, your professional life is not simply something you do to make a living; nor is it separate from your spiritual life as a follower of Christ. It's an expression of who God has made you to be and how he has wired you to thrive in certain areas. That's what is meant when Christians refer to a career as one's "vocation" or calling. As Os Guinness writes in *The Call*, "calling is the truth that God calls us to himself so decisively that everything we are, everything we do, and everything we have is invested with a special devotion and dynamism lived out as a response to his summons and service." Your career is part of your calling, and when you do that task well, you contribute to the flourishing not only of yourself but to the community and society around you.[9]

> Your career is part of your calling, and when you do that task well, you contribute to the flourishing not only of yourself but to the community and society around you.

I can't say that I actually enjoyed scrubbing bathroom tiles or vacuuming floors during my day of punishment for shoplifting. But I did get a brief glimpse of the sense of satisfaction and accomplishment that God has instilled in our souls when we do a job well. For the Christian, work is dignified, and it is an important way that we glorify our Creator and bring healing to the world. Work is indeed worship.

Chapter 2

THE INTRINSIC VALUE OF EDUCATION

WHILE Christians recognize the dignity and value of labor, for most of us, our work is also a key measure of our success in life. The reality is, I could continue scrubbing my bathroom tiles and perhaps gain some satisfaction from that, but if I were doing that task for a living thirty years later, I would not feel very successful in life. That's because, while God created humans to work, we are also wired with a desire to progress in life and to expand the scope of our responsibilities. That's not just a product of our modern capitalist society; the quest to improve, achieve, and expand is also deeply embedded in creation itself.

In the natural world, plants in a garden tend to spread and expand; creatures reproduce and proliferate. The same dynamic occurs on a human level. The apprentice musician masters the violin, and eventually she in turn teaches others. The farmer successfully nurtures the soil and produces crops, and eventually he

> The desire for achievement and advancement is built into us, not just for the monetary rewards but for the satisfaction that comes from being successful in life.

bequeaths more productive holdings to his offspring. The Walmart cashier learns the operations of the store and eventually becomes store manager. Of course, there are dangers in an obsessive drive for greater achievement and more consumption that often characterizes capitalist societies. Anyone who believes in the inherent value of "bigger and better" would do well to read the novelist Wendell Berry to be reminded of the dangers of modern capitalism and the value of being content with one's station in life.

Despite the dangers, however, the desire for achievement and advancement is built into us, not just for the monetary rewards but for the satisfaction that comes from being successful in life. All of which brings us to the main subject of this brief book—education. Pre-modern society was based primarily on agriculture and manual trades. Thus, whether it was working as a farmer, blacksmith, or carpenter, one learned one's craft through apprenticeship. You attached yourself to a skilled craftsman and learned the trade from him until you were ready to strike out on your own. Education too was formed around apprenticeship. Jesus alluded to this tradition when he used the metaphor of apprenticeship in proclaiming, "take my yoke upon you, for my yoke is easy and my burden is light." Even today, much of what is learned in our professions comes through apprenticeship, whether formally or informally. Electricians and plumbers often get their start in the profession as apprentices, and much of what you have learned in your current profession likely came not through formal education but through informal learning from a mentor.[10]

Nevertheless, in our complex society in which many typical tasks require sophisticated thinking and quantitative skills, formal higher education is typically a key component to success in life. So why is furthering one's formal education important to the working adult? Is it worth the hours of sacrifice and the stress of juggling work, family, and school? This chapter will spell out the benefits of higher education for the professional working adult. To do so, and to place education in a proper Christian perspective, it will help to begin by distinguishing between two types of "goods"—intrinsic goods and instrumental goods. An intrinsic good is something that is good simply for its own sake—for example, a beautiful sunset. We don't expect any practical benefits from the sunset; we just value it for its own sake. An instrumental good, by contrast, is something valuable not for its own sake but because it enables us to accomplish something else. Most of us would not mount a Stanley hammer on our living room wall to admire. Rather, we use it to drive a nail. The hammer is simply an instrument to accomplish the separate good of driving a nail to hang a picture, perhaps of that beautiful sunset.

Some things, however, are good both intrinsically and instrumentally. A Stradivarius violin, for example, is valuable as an instrument to play beautiful music. For many, however, the beauty, craftsmanship, and historical significance of a Stradivarius make it an object of intrinsic value, regardless of the music that it creates. A collector who pays a half-million dollars for a Stradivarius may have no musical ability at all. Similarly, my Irish friend has a beautiful hand-crafted Irish guitar mounted on his living room wall. When I visit, I take it down and play it. Physical health has this same sort of dual value. As the nineteenth-century Catholic intellectual John Henry Newman observed, physical health is both an intrinsic and instrumental good: Our bodies are created to be well, and we feel better when we are healthy. Being healthy, however, enables us to achieve other purposes in life such as working, playing, and relating to others.

It is in such a framework that Christians can think about education. Americans are often quick to value education for its instrumental purposes in helping them be more successful in a career. Recently this fact was driven home to me quite vividly when I was driving down a Michigan highway and saw a billboard for a local

> An intrinsic good is something that is good simply for its own sake— for example, a beautiful sunset. An instrumental good, by contrast, is something valuable not for its own sake but because it enables us to accomplish something else.

university with the tagline, "Hire Education." Such professional benefits of a college degree are commonly trumpeted by universities, and they are very real. On average in the U.S., the person who earns a college degree will earn a million dollars more over the course of a career than the person without a degree. And research suggests that during the recent economic recession, the value of a college degree has increased, not decreased. According to Bureau of Labor Statistics, in 2012 the unemployment rate for adults without a college degree was nearly twice as high as for those with a degree.[11]

> On average in the U.S., the person who earns a college degree will earn a million dollars more over the course of a career than the person without a degree.

As Christians, however, we do well to recognize that, first and foremost, learning is an *intrinsic* good, regardless of the practical benefits that it brings. To explore this idea further, let's return to the creation story of Genesis one:

> God created man in his own image, in the image of God he created him; male and female he created them. God blessed them and said to them, 'Be fruitful and increase in number; fill the earth and subdue it. Rule over the fish of the sea and the birds of the air and over every living creature that moves on the ground.'

... And God saw all that he had made, and it was very good.[12]

This biblical creation account has three key implications for education as an intrinsic good.

1. We know God better by studying his creation.

The personality of the sculptor comes through in the sculpture. Similarly, as Creator, God expresses himself in all that he has made, and what he made reveals and declares important things about him. This truth helps us better appreciate why Adam, as representative of humanity, was given the task of naming the animals. Genesis 2 contains this rather startling passage: "Now the Lord God had formed out of the ground all the beasts of the field and all the birds of the air. He brought them to the man to see what he would name them; and whatever the man called each living creature, that was its name."[13]

For the ancient Hebrews, to "name" something meant far more than it does to modern Americans. It meant to understand it deeply, to know the characteristics of the thing named. In other words, God was bringing his creatures to Adam so that Adam could share in God's knowledge of his creation. Adam was to reflect knowing and understanding the animals the way the Creator knows and understands them. In doing so, he would not only reflect the knowledge and wisdom of his Creator, but also know God in a deeper, more profound way. "Naming" a tiger, for example, would help Adam understand and appreciate the beauty and power of God's creation.

Adam's encounter with an otter, by contrast, would teach him something about the Creator's own playfulness and sense of humor. By extension, then, "naming the animals" is what happens whenever we study God's creation. It is what botanists do when they discover a new plant species or what astronomers do when they discover a new galaxy and put a name on it.

When we move from Genesis to the New Testament, we learn that creation itself was the work of Jesus Christ. As Paul writes in his letter to the Colossians: "For by him all things were created: things in heaven and on earth, visible and invisible, whether thrones or powers or rulers of authorities; all things were created by him and for him."[14] To study the created world, therefore, is to study the works of Christ himself.

Because Christians begin the educational task with the understanding that the entire universe is Christ's creation, learning new subjects is never simply about acquiring more information. It's a way to know Christ better and more deeply love him. As John Piper notes, "everything—from the bottom of the oceans to the top of the mountains, from the

> Because Christians begin the educational task with the understanding that the entire universe is Christ's creation, learning new subjects is never simply about acquiring more information. It's a way to know Christ better and more deeply love him.

smallest particle to the biggest star, from the most boring school subject to the most fascinating science, from the ugliest cockroach to the most beautiful human, . . . exists to make the greatness of Christ more fully known."[15] A class in biology isn't just a way to learn about cells; it's a way to deepen your relationship with God, the creator of cells.

2. Education helps us live out the "cultural mandate."

As noted in the previous chapter, Genesis tells us that God intended human beings not just to "name" his creation but to rule over it and develop it. If one of the lessons from the creation account is that humans have been entrusted with the responsibility to care for and develop God's creation, then education helps us to cultivate creation more effectively. The study of engineering, for example, helps us to learn how to build bridges that span rivers. Architecture teaches us how to construct more efficient and comfortable buildings. Graphic design teaches us how to create objects that communicate with clarity and aesthetic appeal. Business helps us develop healthy economic relationships that are essential to any complex society. A course in English helps us use language in creative new ways.

> Of all the creatures, Genesis tells us, humans alone were created in God's image. We alone were created expressly to be like God.

In a host of ways, the subjects studied in college equip us to assume our God-given roles as fellow-cultivators of creation.

3. Education helps us to take delight in God's creation.

Understanding God's creation involves not just the intellect but the emotions. That is because humans were created to experience the same kind of joy and delight in the creation that the Creator himself experiences. God revels in his creation, enjoys it, and loves it. Genesis one informs us repeatedly that God took great delight in his creative activity and called it good. The importance of this truth—God delighting in his creation—is reinforced throughout the Scriptures. In Job 38-41, for example, God tells Job that he plays with large sea creatures; he boasts about the rivers he creates, the storehouses of snow that he keeps, and the understanding he gives to the different creatures.

It is hard to read these chapters and not picture a child at play; but then play also comes from God. Of all the creatures, Genesis tells us, humans alone were created in God's image. We alone were created expressly to be like God. Theologians call this concept the "*imago dei*," the image of God. And while theologians continue to debate the full meaning of this expression, they do agree that it means that we have been uniquely created to understand, to think about, to delight in, and to enjoy the creation the way God does.

Here's an analogy: Picture a father painstakingly constructing a swing-set for his children. His effort is motivated

> One of the intrinsic values of education, therefore, is to help us develop the ability not just to understand but to delight in God's creation.

by the expectation of seeing their joy and hearing their laughter when they jump off the swings and slide down the slide. Their enjoyment of the swing-set not only reflects the father's own affinity for play, but it also expresses their gratitude and admiration for his handiwork. Similarly, when we admire the Grand Canyon, kayak a mountain stream, or cook a savory meal, we express the reality of the *imago dei* and bring pleasure to the Creator of these things.

This concept of human beings created to delight in God's creation provides us with another reason to value education. That's because the beauty of God's creation is not limited to the natural world; we experience it in human culture as well. Poets, artists, philosophers, and even mathematicians discover and develop parts of creation that delight the imagination and feed the soul. I once saw a documentary film about a Princeton mathematician who proved a geometrical concept called Fermat's Last Theorem. He literally broke down in tears as he described the moment of discovery and the "indescribable beauty" and simplicity of the proof.

One of the intrinsic values of education, therefore, is to help us develop the ability not just to understand but to delight in God's creation. A child can enjoy Beethoven's Fifth

Symphony, especially when it accompanies a Bugs Bunny cartoon. But the person who has studied music theory, music history, and the life of Beethoven can appreciate the symphony in a far deeper way. Similarly, the graduate of a course in astronomy can enjoy the beauty of the stars in a deeper way than the person who simply recognizes the Big Dipper in the night sky. In other words, higher education develops our ability to glorify God by enjoying his creation in all of its variety and depth.

In sum, God created all things, and he created us in his image to explore and delight in his creation. Clifford Williams, in his book *The Life of the Mind*, coins the term "living largely" to describe our calling as God's image-bearers. Too many Christians, he says, live constricted lives. They miss the wideness of experiences that comes to those who are open to new possibilities. Living a constricted life is like reading Harlequin romances instead of Jane Austen; or drinking grape Kool-Aid rather than French wine. When we live largely, however, we actively look for fresh ways to experience the richness and goodness of God's creation. In other words, we "image" God better and more deeply as we engage his creation.[16]

> For Christians, education is never simply about career preparation or professional advancement. It is intrinsically valuable and enables us to function more fully as God's image-bearers in the world.

Regardless of the practical benefits of a college degree, at its most basic level, higher education prepares us to image God throughout all of life. God creates; as his image-bearer, I sub-create. Studying art and music enables me to be a better creator. Studying history enables me to better understand how humans have cultivated the "garden" of civilization over time. Every book I read, mathematical equation I wrestle with, or painting I experience expands me and, by extension, my ability to "image" God. Learning economics may or may not make me love God more, but it gives me *more* to love God *with*.

For Christians, therefore, education is never simply about career preparation or professional advancement. Our notion of the universe is deeper and broader than simply material achievement, and so our understanding of education is deeper as well. It is intrinsically valuable and enables us to function more fully as God's image-bearers in the world.

Chapter 3

THE INSTRUMENTAL VALUE OF EDUCATION

As explained in the previous chapter, for Christians, education has intrinsic value as a way to know God better and delight in his creation. For most working adults, however, such intrinsic value is not enough to justify the cost and sacrifice required to pursue a college degree. After all, one can achieve such intrinsic benefits by reading on one's own, watching public television, or participating in one of those free online courses that are proliferating across the internet. The *instrumental* value of a college degree is crucially important if one is to spend considerable time, effort, and money on that endeavor.

To appreciate the practical benefit of education, we need to first understand the unique nature of the modern, complex, globalized workplace—one that makes training for a particular task more problematic than it was a generation ago. Two recent books describe that world and have tremendous

> The instrumental value of a college degree is crucially important if one is to spend considerable time, effort, and money on that endeavor.

implications for higher education today. The first is Daniel Pink's *A Whole New Mind: Why Right-Brainers Will Rule the Future* (Penguin, 2005). Pink tells the story of the past two centuries with a broad but fairly accurate brush. The nineteenth century, he explains, was known as the Industrial Age. New machines were invented that replaced human physical power and produced goods more efficiently than ever before. The changes deeply affected Western society as factories emerged, populations shifted from the farm to the city, and economies increased in complexity. As a result, universities expanded to educate citizens to function more effectively in an industrial society.

In the twentieth century the modern western nations entered a new phase, the Information Age, in which knowledge and information fed the economies of advanced nations. Professions developed, and a new social class came to dominate society—the "white collar" class. The most advanced societies consisted of "knowledge workers" who produced and processed information. For example, factories that produced automobiles could be moved to Mexico where industrial workers were cheaper, but the managers who were needed to plan, develop, and distribute the cars remained in their offices in

Detroit. In such a world, the desirable traits of college graduates were "left-brained" traits such as linear thinking and logical analysis. Law, computer programming, and engineering were the seemingly safe professions that would always provide job security and a good paycheck.

The twenty-first century, however, has witnessed yet another transformation. Advanced societies have reached a level of affluence in which design and aesthetics, not just utility, are desirable traits. In a world of economic choices, consumers want automobiles that are not only practical but aesthetically pleasing. Products that "feel" right, such as the iPad, win out over those that do not. Furthermore, advances in technology and communications, most notably the internet, mean that even complex tasks can be automated and outsourced to other locations. Twenty years ago you would have paid an accountant to prepare your taxes. Now you can purchase and download TurboTax to perform the same function. In the Information Age, a law degree seemingly guaranteed the graduate lifetime job security and a good income. Today, however, the internet is breaking through the information monopoly that has long been the source of security to lawyers. Need a divorce? CompleteCase.com will handle it for a mere $249. In other words, just as machines replaced human power to dig coal shafts in the 1800s, new technologies and global communications today have the ability to replace the knowledge workers of the twentieth century.

Thus, we have entered what Pink calls the Conceptual Age, one in which creators, designers, and collaborators command

> We have entered what Pink calls the Conceptual Age, one in which creators, designers, and collaborators command the highest value. In other words, *creativity*, not computation, is the important trait of the future.

the highest value. The right brain—the part that synthesizes information, sees the big picture, envisions new scenarios, and empathizes with others—is as essential to the modern economy as the left brain. Any computer programmer can write code for an iPhone. But it takes a different sort of mind to envision the need for and value of an iPhone in the first place, and to design one that has that mysterious quality of "feeling right" to the user. In other words, *creativity*, not computation, is the important trait of the future.

There's another important change in the modern world. The programmer writing code for the iPhone—or fielding your phone call when your computer screen freezes up—is more likely to be sitting in a converted warehouse in Mumbai, India, than in Silicon Valley. Such a fact points to another fundamental transformation described by Thomas Friedman in his widely-read book, *The World Is Flat: A Brief History of the Twenty-First Century* (Farrar, 2005). Advances in technology and communications have produced a "flat," rapidly-changing world in which goods are produced through global supply chains and workers in America compete with workers in Russia and China. The typical corporation today is multi-national. The concept for a car may originate in Detroit, but the design plans may be developed in Germany, the parts produced in Mexico, and the car assembled in Alabama. Furthermore, the rise of the internet means that the free market can pinpoint the cheapest labor source, whether that is in sewing garments or writing computer code. In other words, "outsourcing" affects not just factory workers but computer programmers.

A technological, rapidly-changing global economy means that nations at the cutting edge of these changes such as the United States will increasingly find their niche in the "soft" areas described by Daniel Pink. Creative work will continue to occupy a growing segment of the American economy. Of course, we still need people to grow food and build houses. But increasingly, workers in America are expected to do the creative work of research and development, designing new products, and collaborating with workers in other cultures. The modern situation is depicted in the graphic on the following page from the National Center on Education and the Economy.[17]

This is not to say that traditional manufacturing jobs will disappear from the U.S. In fact, recent developments in "lean manufacturing" in the U.S. suggest that the trend of outsourcing manufacturing overseas may reverse itself, at least somewhat. But even the movement toward lean manufacturing reveals the importance of the characteristics discussed by Pink and Friedman. The key advantage of keeping manufacturing

Prototypical U.S. Industry in Ten Years

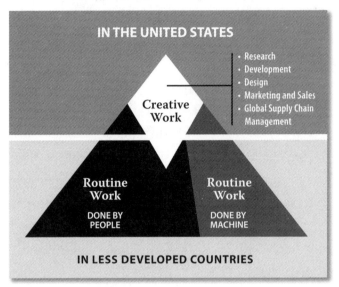

in the U.S. is in creating a shorter, tighter feedback loop between new ideas, their actual production, and their appearance on the market—an advantage that can offset the higher worker wages in the U.S. Thus, the key skills required in a lean manufacturing environment are those of creativity, adaptability, and collaboration with others to make the path from ideas to products as seamless as possible. All of this helps us understand the tremendous value that higher education provides for the adult professional. In particular, higher education develops four qualities that are essential in today's world.

1. Creativity and problem-solving

It almost goes without saying that in our "Creative Age," the ability to think creatively and independently and solve complex problems without close supervision is one of the key traits that a formal education provides. Organizations today need workers who can identify the obstacles to greater productively and clearly assess the various options that are open to them. A course in business statistics, for example, teaches certain mathematical formulas and statistical methods. But more importantly, it teaches the student how to assess various options using hard data, not just hunches or anecdotal evidence. Higher education prepares the professional to see multiple dimensions of a problem and solve it creatively.

That point was made clear recently in "Holistic Engineering," an insightful article by Domenico Grasso, dean of the College of Engineering at the University of Vermont, and David Martinelli, chair of the Department of Engineering at West Virginia University. Because technology is becoming ever more complex and "increasingly embedded in the human experience," they observe, engineers need to think beyond the narrow bounds of their discipline. "A new kind of engineer is needed," they write, "one who can think broadly across disciplines and consider the human dimensions that are at the heart of every design challenge."[18]

Grasso and Martinelli argue that engineers must think holistically for both moral and practical reasons. First, engineering is a discipline that purports to design for humanity and improve the quality of human life. To do so, engineers must attempt "to understand the human condition in all its complexity—which requires the study of literature, history, philosophy, religion, and economics." Furthermore, in a "flat" world where applied technology can be outsourced to Asia, they argue, American engineers need to find their niche as innovative problem *definers*, not just technical problem solvers. Their conclusion: Engineers today must be trained not only in their field but need to develop the ability to think "powerfully and critically in many other disciplines." If such skills are valuable for engineers, they are even more important for businesspeople, educators, health care workers, and leaders of organizations.

2. Adaptability and confidence with change

Imagine the following scenario: You aspire to compete in the Olympics someday. You arrange your lifestyle so that you can become a world-class athlete—you get plenty of sleep, carefully monitor your diet, and of course spend hours a day in training and preparation. But here's the catch: The Olympic organizers have decided that it would be fun to change the Olympic events every four years, and to keep the events secret until a week before the games begin. How would you prepare for the Olympics? Naturally, you would focus on activities that make you as flexible and adaptable as possible. Weight-training would be crucial; but you would not want to bulk up like a Russian weight-lifter because you might be called upon to run the hundred-meter dash. It would be important to develop your hand-eye coordination for table tennis, but also hone your footwork in case you are called upon to do the triple jump.

While such a scenario may be far-fetched in athletics, it's not very far from the world that we live and work in today, and one that you have probably experienced in your professional career. As Friedman notes, in today's globalized, technologically oriented, rapidly changing world, preparing for the future is like "training for the Olympics without knowing which sport you will compete in." Consider, for example, what society was like in the year 2000: Few of us had heard of a radical terrorist group called al-Qaida. Facebook and the iPod didn't exist. About 990 million mobile phones were in use, but the idea of "texting" a friend through one's phone was unheard of. Few Americans would have considered the idea of staying home and having a career as, say, an online content provider or a distributor of goods via the internet. If Americans a generation ago pursued education to be trained as pole vaulters, workers today must prepare to be decathletes.[19]

The value of higher education, therefore, is that, beyond simply equipping the student with a particular body of content or a knowledge of a particular computer program, higher education develops one's ability to learn new ideas and principles, and thus to confidently adapt to the rapid changes that are endemic to the modern economy. When I first began working at a telecommunications software company in the late 1980s, the software language was something called Unix. A college course that taught the basics of Unix would not have much long-term value; but a course that helped to develop my ability to learn programming languages in general would have much more long-term value.

Whether that environment is a traditional classroom or an online class, one of the most important aspects of a college education is not the particular content it provides but rather the intellectual skills of learning new information and techniques which enable the student to adapt to new technologies and situations. The old adage that the purpose of a college education is to "learn how to learn" is more important today than ever.

3. Collaboration and cross-cultural competence

Today's globalized, complex economy means that few organizations or employees function in isolation. Teamwork and collaboration are crucial skills for today's professional. The complexity of tasks means that few individuals control the entire production process of a product; rather, the product is the result of a complex chain of workers and functions. Few organizations have use for the eccentric genius who can design a computer but who cannot work on a team without alienating other co-workers. Moreover, as any business can attest, the changing, globalized economy means that those whom the organization serves are increasingly coming from different cultures or backgrounds. Just ask your local hospital or school how open they are to hiring qualified

> One of the most important aspects of a college education is not the particular content it provides but rather the intellectual skills of learning new information and techniques which enable the student to adapt to new technologies and situations.

professionals who can speak Spanish, Mandarin, or some other language spoken by a prominent ethnic group in their area.

One of the chief values of adult education, therefore, is that it incorporates team-based learning and often exposes the adult student to global perspectives. At my own institution, Cornerstone University, for example, our Master's in Business Administration program requires all students to complete a ten-day Global Business Experience in which they join a team traveling to the Czech Republic, China, Israel, or South Africa to learn business practices in a different culture. Students typically come away from such a trip testifying that it was the most valuable part of their university experience. Regardless of the particular culture, institutions of higher education that prepare the adult professional to function in cross-cultural environments and collaborate effectively with other professionals provide a key quality in today's economic environment.

> One of the chief values of adult education is that it incorporates team-based learning and often exposes the adult student to global perspectives.

4. Knowledge of organizational structures and leading change

Ironically, in today's fluid economic world, institutions become more important, not less. That's because in order

> One of the key values of adult education is that it provides students with an understanding of organizations and how groups of individuals can be assembled and led to accomplish tasks.

for effective ideas to be developed and to take hold in the marketplace, the work, intellect, talents, and resources of countless individuals need to be organized and channeled into those ideas. Thus, our notion of what it means to be creative must expand beyond particular ideas and objects to encompass organizations. As one of the most creative minds of the twentieth century, Steve Jobs, once said, "Sometimes the best innovation is the way you organize a company."[20]

To survive in today's world, organizations need to be structured in such a way that they can adapt quickly and creatively to changes in the environment. IBM was founded in 1911 as a company dedicated to making "business machines." Today it thrives by organizing teams of very smart individuals worldwide to create "business solutions." Kodak, on the other hand, originated as a company to produce cameras. It struggled to re-envision itself as an organization dedicated to providing customers with the ability to preserve the past in images, whether in print or through digital media. IBM successfully organized itself to adapt to change and is thriving today; Kodak did not and filed for bankruptcy in 2012.

One of the key values of adult education, therefore, is that it provides students with an understanding of organizations and how groups of individuals can be assembled and led to accomplish tasks. Back when I was an undergraduate in college, courses such as Organizational Behavior and Principles of Management sounded rather dull. Now that I am a university provost responsible for helping my institution adapt to an ever-changing environment, they sound relevant and interesting. Education is about preparing one for leadership; but leadership happens in particular organizational contexts and processes, and the leader must understand how individuals can be organized and inspired to accomplish tasks in creative new ways. If all Steve Jobs had done was invent a personal computer decades ago, he would be forgotten today. He changed society because he created a company in which a steady stream of brilliant products emerged from the collaboration of creative individuals. Education prepares the professional for success because it develops not just the individual values of creativity but equips the student to understand institutions.

Of all the types of educational institutions, quality universities that are attuned to the adult learner should be the most capable of providing education that focuses on creativity, adaptability, global competence, and organizational know-how.

Of all the types of educational institutions, quality universities that are attuned to the adult learner should be the most capable of providing education that focuses on creativity, adaptability, global competence, and organizational know-how. That's because the adult professional has the life and work experience to recognize that real education goes beyond easy answers and simple formulas. As Sharan Merriam, Rosemary Caffarella, and Lisa Baumgartner observe in *Learning in Adulthood*, younger students often equate college with "informational learning." The adult student, however, generally recognizes that real learning is "transformational" and brings a "fundamental change in the way we see ourselves and the world in which we live."[21]

> Adult learners realize that true education involves personal transformation, and that the real key to professional success is not just factual knowledge but wisdom.

Adult learners have the advantage of bringing more life experience to the educational process, and that experience equips them to value ambiguity and complexity in their educational experience. While traditional students often view the purpose of a college as the simple acquisition of knowledge that will help them land a job, adult learners tend to recognize the importance of higher order learning and collaboration. Mastering a spreadsheet can be learned by just about anyone; learning how to get two employees to collaborate on an accounting project is not so easily done. Adult learners thus realize that true education involves personal transformation, and that the real key to professional success is not just factual knowledge but wisdom.

When I was a child, Campbell's soup ran a marketing campaign designed to appeal both to children and their parents. "Campbell's soup is not just good," the slogan went. "It's good *for* you." As Christians, we can think of higher education in the same way. Because of the doctrine of creation, learning is intrinsically good. God created the world, and he created humans in his own image to understand his creation, to delight in it, and to develop it in new and creative ways.

But being intrinsically good doesn't mean that higher education cannot also be good *for* you. Because God is the creator of all things, at some level "good" and "good for you" blend together. The intrinsically good insights and skills that we acquire as students also prepare us to function effectively in a global economy where creativity, critical thinking, teamwork, and effective communication are vital qualities. Personal transformation is an intrinsic good, but it's also true that wise, creative, and mature adults make the best kind of professionals. A robust, globally focused Christian education is truly good *and* good for you.

Chapter 4

THE CHRISTIAN DIFFERENCE

Adult Education from a Christian Worldview Perspective

So far, we have been discussing the value of higher education for working adults, and much of what has been said applies to both Christian and non-Christian students. While the Christian may appreciate education for both its intrinsic and instrumental value, adult professionals in general recognize the importance of a college degree in modern society. What difference, therefore, does a *Christian* education make, and is there really such a thing as a distinctively Christian approach to education? Isn't Christian education simply teaching and learning that is done by Christians rather than by non-Christians? These are the sorts of questions that I would like to answer in this chapter.

It's important to recognize at the outset that *all* education comes from—and implicitly promotes—a certain point of view, whether we recognize it or not. To understand this important principle, we need to begin with the concept of *worldview.* A

> What difference does a Christian education make, and is there really such a thing as a distinctively Christian approach to education?

worldview is a framework of ideas, values, and beliefs about the basic makeup of the world. It is revealed in how we answer basic questions of life such as, Who am I? Does God exist? What is reality? Is there a purpose to the universe? How should I live my life? It is not so much a set of conclusions based on our experiences as a prior perspective that we bring to those experiences.

Let me illustrate: The popular 1999 film *The Matrix* explored an age-old philosophical question posed by Rene Descartes back in the 1600s: How can I know what is really real? The film begins with the protagonist, Neo, as an ordinary New York City resident. Gradually he becomes enlightened to the true state of reality—that computers have taken over the world and are using humans as power supplies, all the while downloading sensory perceptions into their minds to make them think they are living normal modern lives. Neo achieves "salvation" when he accurately perceives the bad guys not as real people but as merely computer-generated programs.

The Matrix challenges us to recognize that some of our foundational assumptions about reality—that other people exist, that this laptop I'm writing on is really here—are just that: *assumptions* that serve as starting points for how we perceive our world. If my friend chooses to believe that I am a computer program designed to deceive him, it's unlikely that I will be able to produce evidence that will convince him otherwise. Furthermore, as Neo's experience in the film indicates, shifting from one perception of reality to another can be a rather jarring, painful process.

In other words, *The Matrix* illustrates this basic notion of "worldview"—that our prior assumptions about reality shape how we perceive the world around us. We can think of a worldview as a pair of glasses through which we view our world. We do not so much focus on the lenses; in fact, we often forget they are even there. Rather, we look *through* the lenses to view the rest of the world.

A worldview, therefore, is not the same thing as a "life philosophy." A philosophy of life implies a rational, deliberately constructed, formal system of thought that one applies to the world. But worldviews go deeper than that. A worldview is pre-rational, instinctive, and is shaped by my experiences and the community in which I live more than by logical analysis. One could say that my worldview originates in my *heart* as well as my head. It's the means by which I "know" not only that 2 + 2 = 4, but also what

> A worldview is revealed in how we answer basic questions of life such as, Who am I? Does God exist? What is reality? Is there a purpose to the universe? How should I live my life?

the appropriate social distance is in our culture, and that I love my wife. As C. S. Lewis remarks in *The Magician's Nephew*: "What you see and hear depends a good deal on where you are standing; it also depends on what sort of person you are." We cannot help but have a worldview; like the pair of spectacles perched on my nose, my worldview exists and is constantly interpreting reality for me and guiding my actions, whether I notice it or not.[22]

Worldviews shape not just our individual lives but our social institutions as well—which brings me to my earlier contention that all education comes with a worldview. There was a time when many scholars believed that education was completely objective. Professors in the secular academy, it was claimed, simply "studied the facts" and communicated those facts to their students. Now we know better. All education, whether religious or secular, comes with a built-in point of view. Even in academic disciplines, the worldview of the scholar shapes how the data is interpreted, and even what data is selected in the first place. Nothing illustrates this fact better than the following optical illusion often used in psychology courses:

> We cannot help but have a worldview; like the pair of spectacles perched on my nose, my worldview is constantly interpreting reality for me and guiding my actions, whether I notice it or not.

Some viewers immediately see an old lady when they look at this drawing. Others see a young woman. Eventually, just about anyone will be able to see both (if you cannot, relax and keep looking!). This is because, while the actual black and white lines on the page (the "facts," so to speak) do not change, our minds arrange and interpret these lines in different ways to create a coherent whole. Moreover, this is not something that we consciously decide to do; our minds do this automatically. We cannot avoid doing so. Neither can those who visualize the drawing in different ways simply argue objectively about whose interpretation is the correct one, since their disagreement is not so much over the facts of the drawing but over what those "facts" mean.

In a more complex way, a similar process occurs whenever scholars work in their disciplines. Historians, for example, agree on certain events of the American Revolution—that on April

18, 1775, Paul Revere rode through the New England country-side shouting "The British are coming!"; that the Continental Congress signed the Declaration of Independence on July 4, 1776; that on December 25, 1776, George Washington and his army crossed the Delaware River and surprised Hessian soldiers at Trenton. But what do these facts *mean*? How are they to be arranged into a coherent whole? When did the American Revolution actually begin? Was it motivated primarily by religious impulses or by Enlightenment philosophy?

Historians argue constantly over such questions, and the answers to them depend in part on the worldview of the historian, who selects and interprets historical data according to certain assumptions about how politics and societies change—ultimately, basic assumptions about what makes humans tick. Thus, a Marxist historian who believes that ultimately human beings are economic creatures motivated by material rewards will likely interpret the American Revolution in a way that emphasizes the financial self-interest of colonial elites. The Christian who believes that human motivation often runs deeper than just economic interests will likely emphasize other factors such as ideas and religious impulses. The "facts" of the Revolution are the same for each historian, but like Neo's perception of his world, the *interpretation* of those facts is influenced by the scholar's worldview.

It may be easy to see how certain academic disciplines such as history are connected to particular worldviews. It's also the case, however, that universities themselves—even those that are primarily oriented toward adult professionals, are governed by particular worldviews. Moreover, as with individuals, the worldview of a university is typically more implicit than explicit. Universities that emphasize adult education typically orient themselves around the values of personal success and career advancement. Programs are developed in "relevant" fields that will equip adults to become more successful professionally in business, health care, education, technology, and other major sectors of the modern economy. For example, DeVry University's website states: "We believe nothing should stand in the way of you finding success . . . in your education, your career and your life." While not explicitly stated, the worldview assumptions underlying DeVry's programs and philosophy are essentially this:

- Individual success is a crucial value in life that outweighs most if not all other priorities.

- Success is measured primarily in terms of advancement in one's career, which yields greater responsibilities and financial compensation.

- The purpose of higher education is to enhance one's prospects for career success.

From the perspective of most modern Americans, there's nothing necessarily immoral or wrong about such a worldview. From a Christian perspective, however, we may view such an approach to life as shallow and uninspiring, if not morally ambiguous. After all, if "nothing should stand in the way of you finding success," what's to stop you from cheating or stepping on others in order to get ahead? Is there more

> A Christian university seeks to provide a coherent, overarching framework that gives a sense of purpose and unity to everything that it does.

to life than career success? If so, should higher education prepare the student for more than simply career advancement?[23]

In other words, from a Christian perspective, the problem with a secular university is not necessarily that it is ungodly or immoral (though some Christians have argued as much), but rather that its underlying worldview is not robust enough to support the enterprise of education. Moreover, many secular universities make no attempt to articulate and apply an overarching worldview that gives a coherent purpose to all of their parts. As a former college president has remarked, the modern university is not a *uni*-versity at all but rather a "*multi*-versity."

A Christian university, by contrast, seeks to provide a coherent, overarching framework that gives a sense of purpose and unity to everything that it does. That umbrella, of course, is a Christian worldview. Volumes have been written explaining this concept, but for our purposes we can simply think of the Christian worldview as a grand drama in three main acts:

Act 1: Creation. The universe didn't evolve by chance. Rather, an all-knowing, all-powerful, Triune God created everything that exists. God culminated his creative work by making humans in his own image and giving them the capacity to worship him, delight in his creation, and act as sub-creators in their own right. Moreover, God called his creation good and delights in it. Thus, as discussed earlier, all of God's creation is worthy of our study, exploration, and enjoyment.

Act 2: Fall. Human beings, created with a free will, used their freedom to disobey God. Their disobedience distorted our relationship with God, with other humans, and with the created order. As Paul observes in Romans 8, "The whole creation has been groaning as in the pains of childbirth right up to the present time." Thus, all of creation bears the marks of the Fall, from broken marriages to tsunamis that wipe out coastal cities. Everywhere we look in God's creation, we find disorder and corruption of God's original good creation. What we see today, in our own lives, in society, and in nature is not the way it's supposed to be.[24]

Act 3: Redemption and Consummation. After Adam and Eve's disobedience, God immediately set about redeeming his fallen creation and restoring it to its original goodness. The key player in the redemptive drama is Jesus Christ, who came to earth as God incarnate to take the cosmic penalty for sin upon himself. As Paul states in Colossians 1, "God was pleased to have all his fullness dwell in him, and through him to reconcile to himself all things." Eventually history

will culminate in the return of Jesus, who will judge
sin and establish God's reign throughout the entire
universe. In the meantime, the followers of Jesus live
"between the times" of his death on the cross and his
return, extending the effects of God's redemptive activity to every corner of creation.[25]

That's the biblical narrative in a nutshell, and it has tremendous implications for a Christian university. Plants thrive
when they are exposed to a healthy combination of sunlight
and rain. Similarly, we can think of "creation" and "redemption" as complementary purposes that give life to every aspect
of a Christian university.

Take college athletics, for example. A Christian university doesn't just have a college basketball team to boost
school spirit or attract attention, as secular colleges typically
do. Rather, basketball fulfills both a creative and a redemptive
purpose for Christians. God delights in his creation, and he
created human beings in his image to delight in creation as
well. Thus, human play honors God, and developing our ability to shoot a basketball—or spike a volleyball or swing a golf
club—is a way to more fully express God's image.

College sports, however, also bear the marks of the fall.
Athletes are placed on pedestals, coaches sometimes cheat,
and heated contests can degenerate into hatred toward referees and opposing players. A Christian university, therefore, also plays basketball in order to "redeem" this particular
corner of God's creation by fielding teams that demonstrate

sportsmanship and fans who display Christian charity to opponents and referees (that's the ideal, at least).

Of course, most adult students don't care passionately about college basketball—at least not until March Madness rolls around. So let's take an example from a common academic subject in adult education—business. One thing that we learn in the book of Genesis is that God intended for humans to live and function together in community. He also designed his creation to increase in complexity and interdependence. In modern society we see that complexity in virtually every aspect of life. Take, for example, my morning cup of coffee, which would be impossible if I were left to my own resources. The beans for my coffee are grown and harvested on a hillside in Colombia. They are transported to my local grocery store, where I buy a pound of them for a few dollars. The parts for my coffee maker are produced and assembled elsewhere, and the electricity that makes it work is generated by a plant that converts the water flowing from the nearby Grand River into usable power. Simply put, my cup of coffee represents the tip of an iceberg of complex human interactions. And that's a good thing; it's how the world was intended to function.

In its most basic sense, the academic discipline of business is about learning how to efficiently and justly manage the countless economic and social transactions that we depend on each day; in other words, it's about developing our capacity to live out the notion of human interdependence that was part of God's original good design for his creation.

The study of business, however, also has a redemptive component. Unfortunately, economic relations are corrupted by all sorts of individual and structural sin. We see this most obviously, of course, in the corporate scandals that periodically make the headlines. But the effects of the Fall also operate under the radar in economic injustices that might be unwittingly perpetuated even by the coffee beans that I purchase. How does one create a business that pays coffee growers in Colombia a fair price for their beans and still turns a profit in the U.S.? How do communities produce the power needed for their coffee makers while also caring for the environment? How does one responsibly generate wealth and the opportunity to enable others to benefit from good-paying jobs? These are the sorts of questions that courses in business must deal with at a Christian university. In other words, Christians don't just study business in order to advance their careers; they explore how best to practice human interdependence and to redeem economic relations that have been damaged by the Fall.

In sum, every subject that you study at a Christian university has a purpose and value within a Christian worldview

> Christians don't just study business in order to advance their careers; they explore how best to practice human interdependence and to redeem economic relations that have been damaged by the Fall.

framework. I enjoy doing jigsaw puzzles. As anyone who does puzzles knows, the picture on the puzzle box is vitally important. It helps you know where a particular piece fits into the overall puzzle. Without the picture, it would be virtually impossible to put a thousand-piece puzzle together. Similarly, a Christian worldview provides the picture on the puzzle box of a Christian university, helping it to make sense of the various majors, disciplines, experiences, and classes and to arrange them accordingly. It provides the framework that makes a Christian university a coherent and fulfilling enterprise.

Chapter 5

INTEGRATING FAITH AND LEARNING

A Christian worldview animates and gives coherence to a Christian university. But what does that mean for the academic courses themselves that students take? After all, isn't an algebra course simply algebra, regardless of whether one is a Christian or not? Christian educators talk about "integrating faith and learning" in the classroom, a concept that is crucial to a clear understanding of the distinctive value of a Christian university. This chapter will explain that concept and give some examples of integrating faith and learning in some common subjects in adult higher education.

Simply put, the integration of faith and learning means relating one's Christian worldview to an academic discipline. Having said that, it's important to clarify what such a concept does *not* mean. First, integrating faith and learning is not simply a matter of encouraging personal relationships between professors and students. While the nurturing of close

> Simply put, the integration of faith and learning means relating one's Christian worldview to an academic discipline.

mentoring relationships between professors and students is a good thing (and one of the most valuable qualities of a Christian university), it is not what we typically mean by the integration of faith and learning. Such mentoring relationships could—and do—occur at secular and Christian institutions alike.

More than just the relationship between professor and student, the integration of faith and learning affects the actual classroom environment itself. Some Christians have interpreted this to mean that the integration of faith and learning is synonymous with praying before class. While opening class with prayer is a good thing, that's not what is meant by integration. If nothing in the professor's approach to the subject has anything to do with his or her Christian faith after the opening prayer, then a real, substantive integration of faith and learning has not occurred. The opening prayer may simply serve as a convenient tool to quiet students down and focus their minds on the subject.

Finally, some Christians think of integration primarily as a matter of including religious topics within one's area of study. I once attended a lecture by an English professor who explained that when teaching poetry, she used passages from the Psalms as examples of various meters. That's fine, but it's not integration. We would not claim that a Christian carpenter who uses a Bible to prop up a table leg is integrating Christianity and furniture-making. Likewise, professors who simply insert religious material into their classes are not necessarily integrating faith and learning.

Given such inadequate understandings of the integration of faith and learning, it's important to emphasize our initial description of integration as the relation of a Christian worldview to an academic discipline. In other words, it is the ongoing process of understanding a subject in all of its complexity from a Christian perspective, and then to live out its moral and cultural implications. As such, integration involves not just an opening prayer, but the class lecture; and it applies to economics class as well as to Bible class. Scores of books have been written on this subject, but for our purposes we can think of the integration of faith and learning as occurring on three basic levels.

1. The motivational/relational level

The first level of integration draws on some of our observations in previous sections: Our Christian faith motivates us to learn and apply a positive attitude toward the subject of study as a way to grow in our relationship with God. This is integration at its simplest level, but probably the most common level for the college student. For many non-Christians, the purpose of college is quite simple—to do well, get good grades, and assemble an impressive resume for a career. In light of the doctrines of Creation, Fall, and Redemption, however, it should be clear that Christians have a higher purpose and deeper motivation for going to class. Each subject provides an opportunity to know God better, to more fully bear his image, and to become better able to participate in God's redemptive activity in the world.

Let me illustrate concerning the doctrine of creation: A few years ago my son was cleaning out the garage and came across some old spiral notebooks lying in the bottom of a box. They were my journals from my college days. Naturally, he was keenly interested in reading through them and learning more about his father during his developmental years—though I was much more ambivalent about the prospect of my son reading my college journals. Imagine, however, that I had hired my neighbor's son to clean out the garage. He may have been amused at someone's college journals lying around in a garage, but he probably would have had little interest in reading through them.

My son's interest in the journals stems from his relationship to me. I'm his father, and the journals reveal things about his father that he wouldn't otherwise know. In the same way, the doctrine of Creation means that the universe is God's journal

> Christians have a higher purpose and deeper motivation for going to class. Each subject provides an opportunity to know God better, to more fully bear his image, and to become better able to participate in God's redemptive activity in the world.

which reveals things about him that we would not learn in any other way. Our basic motivation for learning biology, for example, stems from our relationship to God as the Creator of the wonderfully complex life forms we study. Moreover, the doctrine of the *imago dei* implies that God equipped us with a natural curiosity about his creation, which we display when we study cells, algebra, or the French Revolution. And if that's not enough motivation, there's also the doctrine

> Integrating a Christian worldview and academics begins with applying a positive attitude toward learning as a means of growing intellectually and spiritually.

of Redemption, which implies that fixing this broken world begins with a better understanding of the problems facing it. Integrating a Christian worldview and academics, therefore, begins with applying a positive attitude toward learning as a means of growing intellectually and spiritually. That can be important to keep in mind for the working adult who is juggling work, family, and school.

2. The intellectual/foundational level

Most Christians would acknowledge that Christian faith should result in a positive motivation toward learning. The integration of faith and learning, however, occurs not just at the attitudinal level but at the intellectual level as well. Because all academic inquiry stems from certain assumptions about the nature of reality, God's existence, human nature, and so on, integrating faith and learning means that we consciously relate our Christian worldview to the area of study. What does psychology look like, for example, to the Christian who believes that human beings are creatures with a soul made in God's image rather than randomly evolved organisms? A course in psychology that integrates faith and learning at the intellectual level will tease out such implications of a Christian view of human nature.

So is there a "Christian" algebra? Not necessarily. When it comes to applying a Christian worldview at the intellectual level, some disciplines will tend to integrate faith and learning more explicitly than others will. There are fewer areas in mathematics where a Christian worldview about the nuts and bolts of the subject is distinctive from a secular worldview than in, say, philosophy, a subject in which one's assumptions about the nature of reality are critical. We can thus think of integration as a continuum. Disciplines such as

> The more that a discipline deals with the nature of human beings and the nature of ultimate reality, the more explicitly worldview questions influence the discourse, since these are questions over which Christians and non-Christians are more likely to disagree.

chemistry focus almost exclusively on physical matter, and as such worldview questions do not typically intrude on the subject. When doing their jobs as chemists, Christians, atheists, Muslims, and others will generally agree about the makeup of molecules and their interactions, despite their different worldviews. Christian scholars may bring different motivations to their disciplines and draw different ethical conclusions from them, but in the actual scholarship itself Christian faith will likely be more *implicit* than explicit.

The more that a discipline deals with the nature of human beings and the nature of ultimate reality, however, the more explicitly worldview questions influence the discourse, since these are questions over which Christians and non-Christians are more likely to disagree. In psychology, for instance, one is never very far from basic worldview questions such as "Do human beings have a soul?" and "What is the basis of human motivation?" In other words, as we move from mathematics and natural science to the social sciences and the humanities, the more explicit one's worldview becomes, and thus more opportunity will exist for the integration of faith and learning, as the diagram below illustrates.

The Implicit/Explicit Continuum

Implicit ———————————————————————————————— *Explicit*

| Mathematics | Natural Sciences | Social Sciences | History | Arts and Literature | Philosophy/ Theology |

Even in the areas toward the left side of the continuum, however, the opportunity for integration never completely disappears. For example, in mathematics, scholars may differ over such foundational questions as, "Are numbers real or imagined?" "Is mathematical truth 'out there' to be discovered or is it invented in the mind of the mathematician?" The answers to these questions are inescapably linked to one's worldview. In the 1930s, Nazi scholars argued that there was a "German" mathematics and a "German" physics, as distinct from "Jewish" mathematics or physics; in other words, that mathematical and physical truth was not "out there" to be discovered but subject to the perspectives of one's race. Their assumptions about race and culture impacted their understanding even of the so-called "hard" sciences.

Recently some psychologists made headlines when they conducted what became known as the "invisible gorilla" experiment. They showed viewers a short video in which a group of people passed basketballs around, and they asked the viewers to count the number of passes made by the people in the white shirts. In the middle of the video, a man in a gorilla suit strolls into the middle of the action, faces the camera and thumps his chest, then leaves. Amazingly, over half of the viewers never saw the gorilla (including myself, the first time I watched it). The experiment demonstrated an important truth: Humans have a remarkable ability to see what they are looking for and not see what they don't look for. Often what scholars "see" in the data is shaped by their worldview assumptions and the questions that they bring to their scholarship. Integrating faith and learning at the foundational level, therefore, means that Christian educators will use their worldview to pose interesting and provocative questions of their disciplines, and to notice things in those disciplines that others may not see.

3. The applied/ethical level

Christianity is not just a way of seeing the world but of *acting* in it. The final way that Christian universities integrate faith and learning, therefore, is by applying the knowledge from a particular discipline to the world in a way that furthers God's creative or redemptive purposes. In other words, it means using psychology to *help* people, not just understand them. But in applying our knowledge, we often encounter ethical questions that cannot be answered apart from worldviews. Einstein's famous equation $e=mc^2$, for example, arouses little debate between Christian and non-Christian scholars. However, when one applies this scientific insight to the development of nuclear energy, all sorts of controversial questions arise. Should we develop nuclear bombs? If so, should they ever be used? What about nuclear power, which provides more energy with less pollution than fossil fuels, but which involves greater risk?

The same can be said for a seemingly "hard" discipline such as engineering. For example, engineers and builders may generally agree that a thinner, lighter window material could save thousands of dollars in material costs when constructing high-rise buildings. However, the cheaper windows may be more likely to blow out during a storm, endangering pedestrians below. At what point does using cheaper windows that

> Integrating faith and learning involves going from a subject itself to working out its practical and ethical consequences for individuals and cultures.

increase the risk of human injury become immoral? The answer to this question depends on the relative value that one places on human beings and therefore human safety—in other words, on worldview questions. Or take the field of journalism: At what point does my obligation as a journalist to uncover the truth of a story conflict with my need to respect the privacy of vulnerable human beings who are made in God's image? Integrating faith and learning involves going from a subject itself to working out its practical and ethical consequences for individuals and cultures.

Integration at the ethical/applied level is common in adult higher education. Indeed, in the most common area of education, business, the ethical issues abound. These occur most obviously at the individual level. For example, as an employee, at what point does my responsibility to tell the truth and act with integrity conflict with my obligation to my employer or to my firm's stockholders? But such ethical issues also occur at a broader level. For example, even if I am behaving ethically in my particular company, is my company itself serving a positive purpose in society as a whole, or is it simply reinforcing the modern values of materialism and consumerism that may be in contradiction to my own Christian faith? How do I determine as a professional whether my institution is furthering God's redemptive purposes in the world or impeding them? For a professional in, say, nursing, the answer may be obvious. For a business professional, the question can be more complex.

When I teach European history to college students, I like to have them read a series of letters between business executives at Topf and Sons, a German engineering company that was responsible for constructing the crematory ovens used at Auschwitz and other Nazi concentration camps. The letters illustrate an astounding truth about human beings—that it's possible even for Christians to simply go about their business as worker bees in organizations and ignore the broader moral dimensions of their work. My work at an advertising agency may not be supporting a Nazi death camp, but might it be promoting in subtle ways a view of human beings as objects to be manipulated for economic gain? If so, how would I know that? While courses in ethics are common in secular universities as well, a Christian university will typically explore the ethical dimensions of a subject at a deeper and more pervasive level.

The integration of faith and learning, then, manifests itself on three levels—the motivational, the foundational, and the ethical. So how does such integration work itself out in practice in adult higher education? To illustrate, I will look at integration as practiced on the ground level in two subjects at my home institution, Cornerstone University.

First, Jim Lacey is a professor who teaches courses in communications at Cornerstone University. Jim's classes abound in "level one" integration. He seeks to get to know the students in his class on a personal level and gives them plenty of reasons to care about the subject. He holds them to high standards, but is also willing to go the extra mile to help them out and assumes something of a pastoral role with them. He even includes his own personal testimony, when appropriate, in his classes.

In addition, Jim integrates his faith and communications at the foundational level by exploring what the Bible says about the subject. He roots the course in God's creation of humans in his image as relational beings who communicate with one another. Finally, Jim integrates faith and learning at the applied level by addressing ethical issues in the field of communications from a Christian perspective, when appropriate. As a result, a course in communications at Cornerstone University engages much of the same material as a course at a secular university, but also incorporates a Christian worldview perspective.

While it may be somewhat easy to see how a Christian worldview impacts a subject such as communications, it also influences a discipline such as statistics, as taught by Cornerstone University professor Jeff Savage. Dr. Savage begins his course by establishing a Christian motivation for statistics. He does so by reading from the book of Nehemiah, which demonstrates the importance of making decisions based on reliable data and using sound reasoning based on that data.

Dr. Savage also integrates at the foundational level by devoting a class session to philosophical and theological issues surrounding statistics. The subject, he explains, tends to privilege a materialistic, reductionist approach to reality, and some proponents seem to believe that whatever cannot be counted quantitatively has no objective reality. In contrast, Jeff establishes a Christian foundation for statistics—that as Christians who believe that God created an orderly universe, we can have faith that we are counting things that really exist and that are orderly and reliable, and we can apply those quantitative results in beneficial ways. At the same time, we know that there are aspects of reality that go beyond the material, and that human beings and human behavior cannot be reduced to statistical data. Furthermore, because human beings are fallen, we must be modest in our conclusions and gracious to those who may disagree with us.

Finally, Jeff challenges his students to integrate faith and statistics at the applied/ethical level by posing moral questions in areas that involve statistical analysis. In fact, in a class that I visited, a student related his family's recent dilemma in deciding

In summary, a Christian approach to adult higher education involves integrating a Christian worldview throughout the academic enterprise.

whether to take his ailing father off of life support, a question that involved, among other things, considering statistical probabilities.

In summary, then, a Christian approach to adult higher education involves integrating a Christian worldview throughout the academic enterprise. Hopefully it fosters quality relationships among faculty and students; but it goes beyond the relational to include the academic subject itself. Of course, such examples of integration don't occur in every class session. As Christians, we can and should ask the big questions of all subjects, but much of our time will actually be spent on the more mundane level of actually learning the discipline. A class on statistics will not get very far if students constantly interrupt the professor to ask, "Are numbers discovered or invented?" While such questions are valid, they won't prevent Christian universities from doing the hard work of understanding the details of the subject itself. Nevertheless, at key points in a course, a professor at a Christian university will challenge students to consider the subject from a Christian worldview and to apply ethical issues from the course to their daily lives as working professionals.

> Higher education isn't the only means to a fulfilling personal and professional life, but for today's Christian adult, a robust Christian college education is certainly worth consideration.

——————— ❖ ———————

I began this book with the story of my own struggle as an adult student to earn an advanced degree while supporting a family. I paid off my graduate school loans by my fortieth birthday—just in time to begin saving for our children's college education! Yet I can confidently say that my education was the best investment that I ever made of my time and resources. Obviously, my degree provided me with the credentials for a career in the field that I love—academia. Even though I rarely teach history in the classroom anymore, the skills, competencies, and insights that I gained in college equipped me for my daily responsibilities as a leader of a university. More importantly, my college education challenged and deepened my Christian faith by enabling me to see the world in all of its complexity as created and sustained by God. And it helped give me a broader purpose in life than academics by connecting my own vocation to God's redemptive work in the world. It was truly a valuable investment that continues to produce benefits. Higher education isn't the only means to a fulfilling personal and professional life, but for today's Christian adult, a robust Christian college education certainly deserves consideration.

ENDNOTES

[1] http://www.studentclearinghouse.org/about/media_center/press_releases/files/release_2012-04-19.pdf

[2] *The Bible*, Matthew 6:33 (all quotations are from the New International Version).

[3] *The Bible*, Genesis 1:28; 2:15.

[4] *The Bible*, I Corinthians 1:26-27.

[5] *The Bible*, I Thessalonians 4:11.

[6] The Epistle of Mathetes, chapter 5 (http://www.earlychristianwritings.com/text/diognetus-lightfoot.html).

[7] Gabe Lyons, *The Next Christians* (Doubleday, 2010), 60. Frederick Buechner, *Wishful Thinking: A Theological ABC* (Harper and Row, 1973), 95.

[8] John Calvin quoted in Allister Stone, "John Calvin, the Work Ethic, and Vocation," *Western Reformed Seminary Journal* 16:2 (August 2009), 24-30.

[9] Os Guinness, *The Call* (Thomas Nelson, 2003), 4.

[10] *The Bible*, Matthew 11:29-30.

[11] http://www.prweb.com/releases/online/MBA/prweb8408122.htm.

[12] *The Bible*, Genesis 1:27-31

[13] *The Bible*, Genesis 2:19.

[14] *The Bible*, Colossians 1:16.

[15] John Piper quoted in Mark Noll, *Jesus Christ and the Life of the Mind* (Eerdmans, 2010), 28.

[16] Clifford Williams, *The Life of the Mind* (Baker, 2002).

[17] National Center on Education and the Economy, "Tough Choices or Tough Times" (http://www.skillscommission.org/wp-content/uploads/2010/05/ToughChoices_EXECSUM.pdf).

[18] "Holistic Engineering," *Chronicle of Higher Education* (March 16, 2007).

[19] Friedman quoted in Jeffrey Selingo, "Rethinking Higher Education for a Changing World," *Chronicle of Higher Education* (July 12, 2006).

[20] Jobs quoted in Walter Isaacson, *Steve Jobs* (Simon and Schuster, 2011), 334.

[21] Merriam, Caffarella, and Baumgartner, *Learning in Adulthood* (Jossey-Bass, 2006), 130.

[22] Lewis quoted in David Naugle, "Worldview: History, Theology, Implications," in Matt Bonzo and Michael Stevens, eds., *After Worldview* (Dordt College Press, 2009), 26.

[23] http://www.devry.edu/whydevry/quality_education.jsp.

[24] *The Bible*, Romans 8:22.

[25] *The Bible*, Colossians 1:19-20.

ACKNOWLEDGEMENTS

As with my previous books, *Reconsidering College* emerged out of my day job as a university educator and administrator. I am grateful, therefore, to my colleagues at Cornerstone University who exhibit professionalism, excellence, and collegiality. Thanks especially to Rob Simpson, Associate Provost of Professional and Graduate Studies, and Sandra Upton, Dean of Graduate Business, for educating me on the virtues and distinctive challenges of adult education.

I am also thankful to Norm Algood, CEO of Synergis Education, for his support in writing this book, and to my president, Joseph Stowell, who continues to affirm my calling to be a writer as well as a provost.

Finally, I am grateful to my wife of twenty-six years, Lonnie, for her love, friendship, and willingness to read my rough drafts to ensure that they make sense to the vast majority of human beings who live and work outside the halls of academia.

Dr. Rick Ostrander
Grand Rapids, Michigan
October 2013